Doggerel Bank

Bank

Comic verses and other nonsense

Brian Long

Illustrations by Jeni Pring

ISBN: 978-1-291-70653-6

PublishNation. London
www.publishnation.co.uk

Raison D'Etre

There are books which tell you how to make a
fortune,
Or teach you how to change your way of life;
And for the more salacious
There are even books, good gracious,
That will show you how to lay somebody's wife.

We find volumes on so many varied subjects,
From tarot cards to large-scale D.I.Y.
Some have subjects esoteric,
Like the verse of Robert Herrick,
Which presumably some students flock to buy.

There are tales of childhood misery and hardship,
Which are meant to be affirming and uplifting;
Often written in a style
That's so overblown and vile
I imagine that they take a lot of shifting.

But this slim volume has no great pretensions,
Though representing my authorial corpus;
Like a restaurant whose dishes
Exclude exotic fishes,
I have to say it serves no useful porpoise.

The Embassy Ball

The "glitterati", no exception,
Were at the Embassy reception;
One fat and pompous politician,
Taking advantage of position,
Sat there replete with food and wine,
And he was feeling rather fine.
As music floated through the air
He gazed around at who was there;
And then he spotted from afar,
Standing alone beside the bar,
A beauteous vision all in red.
He stumbled up to her and said:
"How about a little dance?
I won't give you a second chance."
The vision said, serene and haughty:
"I think that you are very naughty.
I will not dance, for reasons three –
Point one, it is quite clear to me
That you have had too much to drink;
And second, you will find, I think,
The music you are jigging to
Is the national anthem of Peru.
Thirdly, our dance would lead to talk –
I am the Archbishop of York!"

Senility 1

You really know you're getting old
When your wife, your turtle dove
Says:"Darling, let us go upstairs,
And let's make passionate love!"
And you realise with sinking heart
And many a muttered oath.
That much as you may want to try,
You just can't manage both.

Genealogy

Having seen programmes on T.V.
I had myself a mind
To research my own family tree,
And see what I could find.

I'd hoped for revelations –
A pirate, or a King,
But I've gone back generations
And haven't found a thing.

I thought there might be highwaymen,
Some aristos and nobs,
But my kinfolk were serfs, farm-hands
And down-and-outs and yobs.

I found nobody exciting,
No sporting star or pilot –
No hero did the decent thing
And married into my lot.

There was <u>one</u> ancestor of mine
Who fell at Waterloo –
But that was 1989,
And he fell on platform 2.

But now I've found a relative
Who really has some claim
To be remembered, and to give
Our family some fame.

For he died, as fortune chances,
At the battle of Rourke's Drift;
But in the circumstances
He must have been quite miffed.

'Cos he was not of warlike bent,
One of those soldier boys.
He'd just been camping near, and went
To complain about the noise!

The Trouble with Vice is the Price

I would like to indulge in vice,
But at my age can't afford it.
The Chancellor and Ministers
Who always like to lord it
O'er all of us, should make sure that
A portion of our pension
Is earmarked for the purchase of
Things that we never mention –
Like dodgy smokes, illicit sex,
And partying in style,
And pouring liquor down our necks –
It would make life worthwhile!

Drawing a Blank

I honestly don't understand
The purpose of blank verse.
It seems a contradiction,
And really quite perverse;
I can't get my head round it –
It's just a waste of time;
There seems to be no reason,
And certainly no rhyme.
For rhythm, metre, scansion
Are wholly disregarded,
As if poetic principles
Can simply be discarded.
For surely any poem
Should have, from time to time,
At least some lines which end up
With a semblance of a rhyme;
But blank verse lines all seem to be
Inordinately

Terse,
Or else they just ramble on for ages without
actually saying anything much and not ending in
a rhyme anyway.

The Little Nun

As I strolled to my hostelry,
As is my usual wont,
To down a pleasant pint or three,
I heard a voice cry: "Don't!"

I there beheld a tiny nun
In black and white bedecked.
She told me: "Don't go in, my son –
I really do object."

"Beware the demon drink" she raved,
"For alcohol's a sin;
If you are wanting to be saved
I beg you don't go in!"

An imp of mischief made me say:
"I'll bet you've never tried it –
Then how can you be certain, pray,
That I should be denied it?"

"You have a valid point, I know"
She admitted with good grace.
"I should try it, but I won't go
Inside that wicked place."

She said: "No drop has passed my lips,
For 'tis the Devil's brew –
But I should try at least some sips
To prove my point to you."

"I'll buy you one", I then exclaimed
"And bring it out to you –
If after that you feel the same,
Then I'll know what to do."

She said: "One thing before you go;
Please fetch it in a cup –
So any passer-by won't know
'Tis alcohol I sup."

I walked into the pub's good cheer,
The barman shuffled up.
I said: " I'll have a pint of beer
And a large gin, in a cup."

"A cup?" he cried. I answered "Yes."
His eyes flew open wide.
He said: "Don't tell me, let me guess;
That bloody nun's outside!"

Name- Droppers

I was watching a TV quiz show
About classical composers,
And was suddenly reminded
Of one of life's great posers.

Why many of these music chaps,
When they gained success and fame,
Became so very reticent
About having a first name.

We <u>do </u>know all the greats – Wolfgang,
Ludwig, Franz, to name a few,
But for many of the others
We just haven't got a clue.

I think it's a delib'rate ploy;
Guys like Borodin and Hindemith
Just did not like what they were called,
A name that they felt hindered with.

That old curmudgeon Gounod,
Rimsky-Korsakov and Honegger,
Kept it so dark one must assume
They didn't like their monicker.

I don't suppose Camille Saint-Saens
Was keen to have a girl's name,
And as for Bela Bartok,
Well, he probably felt the same.

There's poor old Khachaturian –
Who's surname sounds just like a sneeze;
I doubt that many people
Recall <u>his </u>first name with ease.

On top of Khachaturian,
Which does sound pretty silly,
His parents called him Aram,
As if he were a lily!

Smetana disliked his name –
His story is really a sad one;
And Moussorgsky was too Modest
To admit he ever had one.

Smet'na's father fancied Benjamin
While mother plumped for Frederick,
And so, by way of compromise
They named the poor sod Bedrich.

Young Bedrich really hated that –
Thought the name was so uncool;
He knew he'd be called "Bed" for short
By cruel classmates at school.

He wanted to be hip, with it,
That name made him feel martyred –
'Cos he was streetwise and he knew
Which side his bride was bartered!

I guess people like Ted Elgar
Didn't want their first name shortened,
But others simply dropped it
To make them seem important.

And it's not confined to classics, though,
To music stiff and starchy –
Did anybody ever know
The first name of Liberace?

Swansea, Wales, was the birthplace of Dylan Thomas. Wind Street is a road there, which is full of pubs and clubs, attracting the young. This poem won first prize in the All-WalesComic Verse Competion at the Caerleon Festval 2013.

Under Wind Street

(With humble, mumbled, grumbled apologies to D. Thomas)

Dark night in Swansea Town. Hark! Listen for the staccato stiletto clic-clac down the winding, wounding, curving, swerving, bending, vending length of Wind Street.

Down the road stumble and fumble the Sharons and Kaylees, the Gavins and Daves, half-naked, girls dusted with glitter, boys rampant with bitter, in a noxious whirl of doner kebabs, flaunting abs and ecstasy tabs – scoring, whoring, all bladdered, tights laddered, as Saturday lurches into early, surly Sunday.

The raucous disco turntables cease their dinful, sinful, had-a-skinful spin – blessed silence. In the sudden hush – someone vomits.

Dawn creeps out like a tiptoeing burglar, and the ugly lovely town slips gently back into its boring, snoring, ignoring, closed-dooring
self.

Another bloody awful week ahead.

Valentine 1 - To My Loved One

I think that you'd be very mean
If you won't be my Valentean –
I love you in so many ways,
It really isn't just a phays.
I'd come to you though hail and rain
If you would be my Valetain,
And I would be prepared to sue
If someone said I don't love yue.
The Foreign legion I may join
If you won't be my Valentoin.
I offer you my hand, my heart
And also every other peart –
So please agree that you are mine
And that you'll be my Valentine.

Senility 2

Asked about sex at seventy-five
I say: "It's fine for me,
Because I only live next door,
At number seventy-three!"

Stay out of the Garden, Maud

My wife's become a gardener –
It happened all at once.
In all things horticultural
She used to be a dunce;
But now she's really got the bug
(Or sprayed the bug away).
She's pottering and potting out
For eighteen hours a day.

My wife's become a gardener,
As strange as it nay seem –
She used to think hydrangeas
Were a Scottish football team.
She always used to say, like me,
The most idyllic scene
Outside the house would be a strip
Of concrete, painted green.

But now she is a gardener –
I may well have to leave her;
She fills the house with flowers
Which play hell with my hay fever.
She used to rest on our chaise-longue,
Relaxed, in casual poses;
But now she's out in gumboots,
Deadheading all the roses.

My wife's become a gardener –
She's out in sun and rain.
Our water bill's approaching
The national debt of Spain.
Our cat doesn't support me –
He sits out there and purrs;
'Til she nearly took his ear off
With a pair of secateurs.

I think, now she's a gardener,
To make myself endearing,
I'll bury myself in the garden
With just my head appearing.
At least she then might notice me
And our love will endure –
But more likely I'll end up
With a faceful of manure.

Journey's End

Near midnight, as the port went round
We fell to musing on
The prospect of our own demise,
When our lives would be gone.
We all agreed a painless death
Would be the ideal thing –
No agonies of pain and fear,
No long-drawn suffering.
I said: "I think I'd like to go
Just like my Uncle Jim;
One day he simply fell asleep,
And that was it for him".
And that's the way it ought to be –
No panic, pain or fuss,
Nor screaming out in abject fear
Like the passengers on his bus.

The Sad Fate of Charlie Dickens

It's a little-known fact that Charles Dickens
Was dyslexic as a youth –
And his earliest works were all failures,
To tell you the absolute truth.

As an instance, most people found "Hard Tomes"
Very difficult to read –
And "The Adventures of Oliver Twat"
Pleased very few readers indeed.

His novel called "Grate Expirations"
Caused ladies to wail and to weep;
They'd expected a romantic story
Of a poor dying chimney-sweep.

His "Arnaby Bridge" never was found
(of course, they had no GPS),
Which probably was the main reason
That it wasn't a roaring success.

And finally the poor chap's dyslexia
Brought about his fall from grace –
Gave Victorian elite apoplexia;
He could scarcely show his face.

The eventual cause of his downfall
Made even his best friends withdraw;
When he wrote "A Sale of Two Titties"
That must have been the last straw.

Men versus Women
(If you don't want to know the result, look away now)

It's just anathema to me, this battle of the sexes –
I don't know why it still goes on, it puzzles and
perplexes.
It's full of generalities, old-fashioned stereotypes,
Espoused by idiot men who think themselves
superior types,
And fanatic, angry harpies, who think men
overrated,
And wouldn't be that bothered if we were all
castrated.
Why don't we simply celebrate the qualities we
share?
The things we have in common – abundant, rich
and rare.
So calm yourselves, you angry folk, as at your
bits you champ.
You want to air your diff'rences ? Go to a nudist
camp!
On second thoughts there <u>are</u> some things which
show us far apart –
Like woman's need to chatter, and man's equal
need to fart;
And girls can't leave a fashion shop without
fondling every sleeve,
While men, after we've used a loo, the seat
upright must leave.

I don't believe the saying old: "Men are from Mars, women from Venus"
No, women are from M and S, and men from Planet Penis.
I guess the nearest thing to truth, known to us all along,
Is "Woman's place is in the home – and man's is in the wrong".

Valentine 2 – Going from Bard to Verse

It's tough to find new things to say
To celebrate this special day.
I've sought assistance from the Bard
But even he would find it hard;
I've looked up Longfellow and Shaw,
Byron, Ted Hughes and Evelyn Waugh –
Read Shelley,Tennyson and Dryden,
But still my muse seems to be hidin'.
I even (could it get much worse?)
Consulted those two giants of verse –
Poets whom the text-books chronicle:
Spike Milligan and the great McGonagall.
I'd gladly give a cask of wine
For one new rhyme with "Valentine"-
Well, maybe not a cask, a pichet,
For something that is not a cliché.
This versifying is a pain,
And is, I fear, this time in vain.
The only thing that I can say
Is that I love you more each day,
And that my life will be just fine
If you will be my Valentine.

Nature's Gentleman

Now of all the creatures in this world,
Which would we deem most gentle?
Even the cuddly, furry ones
Which make us sentimental,
Have armouries of teeth and claws
Which are enough to give us pause.

The ocean-dwellers can be fierce –
Even a sea-anemone
Can muster some defences
If it sees you as an enemy;
And if you're really out of luck
You'll end up with a nasty suck.

Some animals are clearly out
Of such a competition –
It's no good lions, tigers, bears,
Jockeying for position;
Cheetah, for all his fearsome pace,
Is a 'non-runner' in this race.

What we are really seeking is
A creature who's so meek and mild
We'd leave them with impunity
With even quite a tiny child,
And not risk coming back to find
Just half a baby left behind.

We wouldn't want to chance upon
A pile of fresh entrails
And have to clear up bits of bone
With all which that entails,
Nor face finding a tiny limb
Formerly part of her(or him).

But no more of this gruesome talk;
Of the victor there's no doubt –
An animal whose peaceful ways
We've always known about.
It's all embodied in a phrase
Known to us from our childhood days.

When young, we often heard it said,
By Mum or Dad, or both,
When they have been comparing us
To another mild creature, the sloth;
That after all is said and done
Aardvark never hurt anyone!

The Last Lay of the Minstrel

"How do I love thee ? Let me count the ways
….."
To be quite frank, there's really only one way
nowadays;
The overwhelming problem which affects us day
and night is
A mixture of excessive weight and galloping
arthritis.
So all that we can manage in our pitiable
condition
Is what is rather oddly called "the missionary
position".
No more the fine old frenzy of our youthful
sexual tangles,
Encountering our naughty bits at unexpected
angles.
But I will tell you something which may help the
blow to soften;
I love you every bit as much – if maybe not as
often.

*Publisher's note: This is a work of fiction; any
resemblance to any persons living or retired is
entirely coincidental (by the way, apologies to
Walter Scott and Mrs. Browning, too).*

Senility 3

Life is horticultural
I think, in my old age;
While younger people sow wild oats
The elderly grow sage.

A Fishy Tale

The gourmets of New England,
The diners of Cape Cod,
All clamour for one delicacy,
The curiously named "scrod".
It seems a most unlikely name –
A word which one might babble
When influenced by alcohol,
Or trying to cheat at Scrabble.

But no, the scrod indeed exists,
A prince among all fishes –
And North Americans insist
It is the most delishes.
So woe betide a restaurateur
Who serves a plate of salmon.
It may be sent directly back –
That's really not uncammon.

And furthermore, t'would also be
A very big mistake
To try to tempt these customers
With a tasty piece of hake.
And as for more exotic types,
Like sild or barracuda,
The normally mild Bostonian
Could scarcely be much ruda.

And anyone who foolishly
Offers a meal of tuna,
Would soon find that their clientele
With one accord, would soona
Depart at once, in dudgeon high,
Old, young, and even toddlers,
And seek another place to dine
Rather than go home scrodless.

So when I was last in Boston
I approached a local "plod"
I said: "Excuse me, Officer.
But where can I get scrod?"
At first it seemed his answer
Didn't make a lot of sense –
He said: " I've never heard that word before,
In the pluperfect tense."

I'm Just Not Very Ept

I was standing at the mirror
Getting ready for a date;
I'd bought a bunch of garage flowers
And a box of After Eight.
Without the evitable doubts
Which usually bedevilled,
I thought that I looked nicely kempt
And really rather shevelled.
My hairstyle was behaving,
And I was thinking truly
For once I did look pretty smart
And absolutely ruly.
The day was clement, fine and warm,
And I was feeling couth,
And then in came my brother,
Who is a charmless youth;
With a cold sneer which wasn't ane,
He said: "You look a mess".
I realised that he was right –
It caused me some distress.
In one fell swoop he'd broken down
The image I had mantled,
Leaving me feeling insecure
And very far from gruntled.
It really brought me down to earth
To see myself so plainly;
'Cos up to that point I had thought
That I looked pretty gainly.

I'm A Librarian, Get Me Out Of Here

Surrounded by impressive tomes,
By ageless novels, plays and poems,
I sit until my work is done,
And skim the pages of the "Sun".
My "War and Peace" is still pristine -
I never got past page fifteen;
I have a set of Edward Gibbon,
Unopened, still tied with a ribbon.
I've just no interest at all
In his, or Waugh's "Decline and Fall".
I told myself I should read Proust,
To give my intellect a boost:
"A la Recherche du Temps Perdu"
Or as it's known to me and you:
"Remembrances of Things Past"-
But then I thought: "I can't be arsed!"

Nor modern writers of renown -
Best-selling authors like Dan Brown.
Far-fetched adventures on the road
To D'Vinci's secret left me "code"
I didn't even open that
Because it's such a load of tat.
I honestly don't give a toss
About the old "Mill on the Floss"-
I couldn't care less what befell
Dickens's poor Little Nell,
Or Berniere's Captain Corelli -
I'd really rather watch the telly.
I'm not some thick uncultured yob,
I'm just in the wrong blooming job.
'Though it may bring me dirty looks,
I must confess - I don't like books!

Apposite Adverbs

"Do you have to play C.Ds at this hour?" Tom said disconsolately.

"I've stopped wearing jewellery", said Sue endearingly.

" I'll have the steak and kidney", he said piously.

"This is my boyfriend", she said urgently.

"I collect stamps", he said flatly.

"I'm from a town in South Wales", she said carefully.

"Just two more and I will have made a dozen sets of false teeth", he said tendentiously.

"I always wear denims", she said ingeniously.

'That's the daftest thing I ever heard", he said superciliously.

" There's a convict escaping over the wall", she said condescendingly.

Senility 4

I know old age is coming on
As, sadly it emerges -
I've started getting symptoms
Where I formerly had urges.

Ode for Saint Dwynwen's Day

Today is the feast of Saint Dwyn
Wen red-blooded Welshmen should join
In praising their sweethearts and wives,
And telling them how much they enhance our
lives.
'Tis the time to keep all of them sweet,
And pray that the sweethearts and wives never
meet.

Well, That's It

I hope this book has given you
A laugh, a chuckle, smile –
And that it proved a pleasant way
Some time away to while,
But whether you lock it away
For children to inherit
Or seek to bin it 'cos it has
No literary merit
You should be told it was designed
To serve a dual purpose
(I guess because the publishers
Thought there would be a surplus).
It's all been carefully thought out,
With usefulness in mind –
Dimensions, cover, thickness,
Are perfect, you will find
To serve its secondary role
And easily enable
Its usage as a handy wedge
For a wobbly café table.